52 SALES MANAGEMENT TIPS

THE SALES MANAGER'S SUCCESS GUIDE

STEVEN ROSEN

Published by:
STAR Solutions That Achieve Results Inc.
20 Pickett Crescent,
Richmond Hill, Ontario
Canada
L4C 9K9
Website: http://www.starresults.com
E-Mail: steven@starresults.com

To my wife Betti,

for giving me two amazing kids,

a loving home

and endless support.

Table of Contents

52 SALES MANAGEMENT TIPS

Praise for 52 Sales Management Tips:

Wow, Steven has got it right...Focus on *sales management* to increase *sales* performance. No complicated strategy, just actionable coaching tidbits that guide you to the right tool for the right situation at the right time. You will be amazed at how you can tackle so many management issues in so few words...52 times. This book is a must for the sales management professional.

William "Skip" Miller, author, ProActive Sales Management

"The sales manager is the pivotal person in the sales-driven organization, and Steven's book shows you how to excel!"

Brian Tracy, author, Getting Rich Your Own Way

"52 Sales Management Tips is a must read for any front line sales manager or for anyone aspiring to be a front line sales manager! Sadly over the last 30 years there has been a documented decline in the professional

1

development of front line sales managers by too many corporations.

52 Sales Management Tips is short, concise, relevant and insightful. Follow Steven's advice, implement 1 tip a week and watch your people transform while sales soar!"

Andy Miller, Founder and Senior Partner, Big Swift Kick

"In 52 Sales Management Tips, Rosen offers practical, actionable tips for sales managers to "up" their game. By acting on these tidbits of wisdom, you'll see a big difference in your sales results."

Jill Konrath, author, *SNAP Selling* and *Selling to Big Companies*

"The role of the sales manager is far more important than the sales profession realizes. Fortunately, Steven Rosen has written a "go-to" book for sales managers looking to improve their skills. I'm recommending this must-have reference guide to the sales managers I know, so that they can begin today to be better

2

equipped for any challenges and opportunities that come their way."

Mark Hunter "The Sales Hunter"

"Few if any (until now) sales books on the market currently address one of the most critical elements for consistent sales success, specifically the front line sales manager. Steven Rosen's brilliant book is concise, to the point, and most importantly executable. It is a fact that the ROI on a dollar invested in front line sales manager is much greater than a dollar invested in sale reps, your first investment to maximize your returns should be in this book."

Tibor Shanto, Principal – Renbor Sales Solutions Inc.

"Steven has put together a concise handbook that's easy to understand and applicable. Steven's expert gems are truly golden for sales managers wrestling with hiring, training and coaching sales people, managing customers and winning business and managing executive expectations all at the same time."

Craig Klein, President/CEO Sales Nexus

"Time is of the essence in today's workplace and in this quick and definitely easy-to-read book Steven Rosen shares his own 20 plus years of executive coaching. Steven uses his personal sales experience to create a guide full of common sense with a dash of humor (see tip #26). This book is an action springboard for those sales managers regardless of experience level who are seeking simple changes that will quickly translate into sustainable sales success."

Leanne Hoagland-Smith, CRO & Founder of ADVANCED SYSTEMS

"Steven has written a great book with many ideas that can turn a good sales manager into a great one. If you will just concentrate on effectively implementing one idea a week into your leadership style by the end of a year's time I am 100% certain your results will be incredible."

Jerry Acuff, CEO and founder of Delta Point

"Steven has put 52 of the most important actions and behaviors of top sales coaching into one concise book! Steven's book reminds me of some of the behaviors I need to exhibit to be the best coach I can! These 52 tips should be on the top of your desk!"

Jim Hughes, Sales Leadership Consulting

"Any sales manager, whether he/she is newly-promoted, or a seasoned veteran, will get valuable, instantly-useable ideas in Steven Rosen's **52 Sales Management Tips**. It's not a book to just be read once, review it regularly to take advantage of all the wisdom shared from Steven's 20 years of experience."

Art Sobczak, author, "Smart Calling-Eliminate the Fear, Failure, and Rejection from Cold Calling."

"If there's one thing that's more difficult than selling, it's managing people who sell. In this practical book, sales guru Steven Rosen reveals one sales management tip for every week of the year. Follow Steven's suggestions and I can confidently predict that your sales figures will rise sharply."

David Straker, author, "Changing Minds"

"When Steve asked me to read his book I jumped at the chance. He has created an ideal handbook for sales leaders, jammed packed with concise ideas and tips for all sales managers. I believe Steve's book should become a "field guide book" for sales management. Carry it with you everywhere! Read it 3 times to capture all the insights and then re-read every 6 months!"

Ken Thoreson, author, Your Sales Management Guru series, Acumen Management Group

"Steven Rosen actively coaches sales executives and sales managers' to drive performance through people. His new book, **52 Sales Management Tips** (why the subtitle? Lose it, it seems artificial) is packed with pearls of wisdom that will help any sales leader take their game to the next level. If you lead a sales team, Steven's practical and tactical sales management tips will help you to inspire your team and drive more sales."

Dr. Tony Alessandra, author, The Platinum Rule for Sales Mastery and The NEW Art of Managing People

"Steven Rosen, one of the top sales coaches I know, has written a phenomenal book for sales managers' that has the power to transform their professional lives. Steven has expounded on 52 of *the* most vital actions a sales manager must pay attention to, in order to be successful. This is a book that will help you with hiring, coaching and training salespeople and produce more business than you ever imagined. It's a quick, fun read that you won't be able to put down. If you want to be a great sales manager, Steven wrote this book for you!"

Robert Terson, author, Selling Fearlessly

"Congratulations Steven on "**52 Sales Management Tips**". You have put together a guide that's easy to read, filled with practical tips that help sales managers succeed in becoming more effective and productive in the job of sales management. I recommend this book to all sales managers!"

Domenic Maccarone, Senior Director, Sales, Lundbeck Canada

"I very much enjoyed Steven's **52-Sales Management Tips**. He has a practical and straightforward approach to sales management. I feel his lessons are a must read for any first-time people manager, and a great reminder for those who've been leading sales teams for years."

Stu Fowler, General Manager Allergan Canada

"Steven Rosen nailed it with **52 Sales Management Tips**. Front-line sales management is an incredibly difficult job with different constituencies pulling you in every direction. Senior executives want one thing, customers another, and your own team is all-to-happy to steal your time. Rosen's book brings much needed outside perspective to help you lead, set the agenda and take back control of your calendar. It's easy to read, well laid-out and gushes with practical, actionable tips. Get it!"

Mike Weinberg, Sales Consultant, Coach and Author of the Amazon Bestseller *New Sales. Simplified.*

Forward:

My name is Tricia Symmes. I am a senior pharmaceutical sales and marketing executive with over ten years of experience. My goal has always been to continually grow my leadership skills and drive sales performance. To this end, I found an executive sales coach named Steven Rosen.

In working with Steven, I have had the opportunity to grow both professionally and personally. As an executive sales coach, Steven has been instrumental in providing valuable advice on very challenging and complicated business cases ranging from coaching, to managing performance issues and to navigating the boardroom.

A good coach in my opinion should be a consummate listener and an accurate diagnostician. A good coach teaches his clients how to work through issues and to develop strong solutions. A good coach provides practical and immediately applicable tips that can be put into action and render positive impact on performance. Steven Rosen is a GREAT coach.

Over the past seven years, Steven has worked with me on how to quickly diagnose issues and address those issues. I have learned how to better mentor, support and coach my own teams to excel as leaders. I have learned how to be my own best leader.

A good mentor should push you and they should not provide the answers but rather provide you with the tools and tips to address issues yourself. My coach, Steven Rosen has challenged me to grow both personally and professional. I just had to learn how to access my inner coach!

Steven has helped me focus on how to challenge the status quo, how to influence others and the importance of teaching my people how to "fish" for themselves. He encouraged me to take risks, become a shrewd negotiator, understand better the boardroom politics and develop strategies to move my business forward.

My team has been impacted in ways we never anticipated. He pushed my people outside their comfort zones. Steven took my top players and stretched them to new levels of performance. We all quickly became accountable for our plans, performance and strategies. As a consequence, confidence levels were raised, abilities to make astute business decisions were magnified and there was a vast improvement in the handling of difficult situations and challenges.

I have had the opportunity to recommend Steven to many colleagues. All of them have said to me, "Thank you for introducing me to Steven, he is phenomenal and has helped me become a stronger leader." He has been the best coach I have had the pleasure to work with in the last 14 years of my career in sales management.

My favorite tip in his new essential coaching guide, **52 Steps to Sales Management** is Tip #17 "Trust your Instincts."

I hope you read Steven Rosen's book cover to cover. And then I hope you start employing his many useful and essential tips to help you become the best sales manager that you can be.

Good luck coach!!

Tricia Symmes
Vice President, Integrated Hospital Care and Critical Care
Novartis Pharmaceutical Canada Inc.

Introduction:

Thank you for picking up **52 Sales Management Tips: The Sales Manager's Success Guide**. You have just taken the first step towards changing your life. This book is designed for sales managers who struggle within a corporate environment that doesn't always support them or their development needs. Whether you are a sales executive, senior sales leader or a new, experienced or aspiring sales manager I'm confident you will find this book to be a valuable guide to consult whenever you are experiencing problems.

Front line sales managers are facing unprecedented change. Managers are dealing with increased demands to do more with less and are still expected to drive sales performance. With little support from the next-line of sales management and a lack of relevant courses and ongoing development you may feel stretched to the limit.

Your role is paramount to the success of your organization. Front line sales managers are the key to unlocking the potential of the sales force and driving sales performance.

Here's why:

1. The #1 performance factor for sales people is the quality of their manager. A high quality manger has far greater impact on performance than skills training or compensation.

2. The #1 manager activity associated with rep success is coaching. Coaching is the single most impactful activity that front lines sales managers perform. Studies show that effectual coaching can impact sales performance by as much as 20%!

3. The #1 reason why top performing sales reps leave an organization is their relationship with their manager. Great front line sales managers do a better job retaining top performing sales people than mediocre managers.

Most CEO's recognise the upside of coaching and yet are still reluctant to embrace change. The fact is most organizations don't invest sufficient funds to support the growth and development of their front line sales managers. As a result, corporations are not reaping the true value from their investments in sales forces and the numbers continue to decline.

I have coached dozens of front line sales managers and have seen firsthand, the impact they can have on performance if given proper support and development.

Overworked and under-supported front line sales managers are desperately looking for resources to improve their performance. This book was written for sales managers who understand the need to develop themselves. They have figured out that they must take charge of their own success.

For this book, I distilled over 20 years of my sales management, sales executive and sales executive coaching insights into one simple reference guide. I am always amazed at the positive reaction I continually receive when I share these tips with the sales leaders that I coach. Once you begin, you will immediately begin to benefit from my experience coaching mediocre managers into "star sales leaders." You, yourself will become a sales leader to follow.

That's the reason why I wrote **52 Sales Management Tips**. It is my hope that the insights I share will help you with the many challenges you face in your workplace. I have carefully chosen my 52 top tips based on recurring themes I have seen with my coaching clients. Over and over again, I find myself quoting from my list of tried and true tips. After a while, I have realized that I could extend my reach and create a book to share my tips with a wider audience on coaching to excellence.

I have found that sales managers struggle the most with how to:

    1. Be a more effective coach
    2. Handle their boss
    3. Hire sales STARS
    4. Drive sales performance and
    5. Manage different types of people

This book has my top 52 tips of what to do as a sales manager. It is intended to provide provoking, inspiring and witty insights from my 20 years of extensive experience in the area of sales management. My goal is to share with you a year's worth of weekly tips to guide you to success.

I understand that many of you are busy and like me have short attention spans. This book doesn't read like a novel. I have taken my best insights and shared them with you in a concise, easy to read format. My goal is not to lecture or speak theoretically. I want to share with you my best practical tips, the nuggets of truth that will provide you with the know-how in how to succeed as a sales manager.

My bet is that you are going to want to read this book cover to cover. Each tip can be implemented immediately or stored for future use when a situation arises.

I have helped many sales leaders and front line sales managers' breakthrough, and I can help you as well. I want **you** to achieve the success you desire in a sales management role. Time and time again the top sales managers are able to drive sales performance through people. Managers, who can effectively help their sales people improve, will rise to the top. Let the tips in this book be a guide to your success.

I hope you enjoy reading my book and that it inspires you to be the **best** sales manager you can be.

Chapter 1: Becoming "GREAT"

"The task of leadership is not to put greatness into people, but to elicit it, for the greatness is there already."

John Buchan, Scottish politician, author (1875-1940)

Chapter 1: Becoming GREAT

The first chapter focuses on my tips to becoming a great coach. The most important factor for success for any sales manager is to develop their sales team to be the best. Coaching is the most important skill to effectively develop top sales performers. What I have found is that many sales managers have never learned how to be effective coaches.

There is little or no training on coaching. Sales managers who receive coaching training often fail to translate their training to on the job skill enhancements. The problem is that the next level of sales management often fails to role model and reinforce the coaching techniques.

In this section you will learn my top tips on how to effectively coach. Read them, process them, and apply them and you will see a definite improvement in your coaching practices.

Tip #1: Just Do it

If sales results are what you desire then do the activities that will drive the greatest sales. The two sales management activities that generate sales are

1) attending meetings and conferences with clients and 2) coaching sales reps. Research shows that managers who spend more time coaching generate significantly more sales.

Make coaching your #1 priority! Your boss will thank you and your reps will make lots of money.

Tip #2: Start Asking

Stop telling your sales people what to do. A great sales manager asks effective questions. Effective questioning forces reps to come up with their own solutions and improve their performance. Effective questioning creates self-awareness and self-managing salespeople.

Warning: Don't be one of those managers who think they are a "Super Rep" by continually solving your sales reps issues!

Tip #3: Coach One Step at a Time

The key to developing a stronger team is to FOCUS on improving one competency at a time. This may seem like baby steps and may take several months to a year to accomplish, but you will end up with marked improvements in those competencies overall.

Be careful not to try to improve too many competencies all at once, as you will end up making no impact at all.

Tip #4: Understand "Why"

When coaching sales people it is critical that you understand the reason "why" a goal is important. The why is the internal motivation that will drive the sales reps to achieve their goals. It does matter whether they are motivated by pride or sense of success. If you as their manager/coach can tap into the why, you will be much more effective at appealing to their internal source of motivation and help them achieve their desired outcome.

Tip #5: People Respect What You Inspect

Make sure you inspect important tasks that you expect your reps to do. For example, when you ask a rep to send you their plan on achieving a specific goal you need to hold them accountable to deliver on your expectations. Take the time to review the plan. Follow through on your end. Your rep will respect the effort and rise to meet your expectation.

Tip #6: The Power of the Pen

To increase the chance that your sales reps will achieve a goal they have set for themselves it is critical to have them commit their plan to paper, write it down! When people put pen to paper it has two key benefits. Firstly, they have thought out what specific activities/steps they need to do to achieve their goal(s) and secondly the process of writing crystallizes in the brain what they intend to do. This speaks to commitment. With a written commitment the sales rep takes ownership of the outcome.

Tip #7: If it's to be, it's up to the "Coachee"

If you want your sales people to improve their skills and make more money, you must coach them to success. But if someone doesn't want to change, grow or improve, there really isn't a whole lot you can do. The coaches' role is one of facilitating and holding the individual accountable to the agreed upon actions involved in the coaching process. The effort required for growth and change is up to the individual, not the manager.

You can't coach someone that doesn't want to be coached! So don't waste your time with the uncoachables.

Tip #8: Customise Your Coaching

Coaching is a "one to one" sport. It has to be specific and delivered in a way that best speaks to the individual.

Coaching is not training. Coaching is about diagnosing each sales reps particular area for improvement. It is about adapting your coaching style to the person and about developing individualised development plans. It is unique to each individual rep.

Don't be one of those managers who coach all their reps the same way. If you do, then you have fallen into the trap of "one size fits all" coaching.

Tip #9: Don't Pursue Sales Results

The pursuit of sales results is important. Although sales results are short term, STAR sales managers pursue results by focusing on developing their sales people to reach their true potential. By developing your people, you get improved performance and better retention, thereby developing a pool of top performers.

Develop your people and sales results will follow.

Tip #10: Owning it!

Buy-in is key for change/growth. If your sales reps want to improve a specific competency it is critical that they develop their own multi-point plan on how to do so. Managers who tell their reps what to do will have limited impact.

Have your sales rep develop a 3 point development plan of action. When it's their own idea you will get both commitment and buy-in.

Tip #11: Focus on the Middle for Performance

Coaching is neither a democracy nor a communistic activity. Spending equal time with each rep does not give you the biggest bang for your buck. The group that provides you with the best impact from your coaching efforts are your core performers. Focus a greater effort on your core performers to drive peak performance.

Do you know what GREAT coaching looks like?

Chapter 2: Managing Challenge

"Effective leadership is putting first things first.
Effective management is discipline, carrying it out."

Stephen Covey, author, *The 7 Habits of Highly Effective People*

Chapter 2: Managing Challenge

Sales managers have no shortage of challenges. The workplace is becoming more and more complicated. You may be facing a myriad of obstacles blocking your success such as managing a boss, managing time commitments and job delegation, just to name a few. This chapter will help you navigate and effectively overcome many difficult situations.

One of the key solutions is proactivity. If you have the know-how and energy to address these different challenges and meet them head on, you will not only survive but you will thrive.

Tip #12: Proactively Manage your Boss

Your boss is no different than you. All bosses want to know two things: one, that you know what your issues are and, two, that you are doing something about them. Put yourself in your boss's shoes. S/he has enough to worry about. If your boss is spending time wondering what you are doing about your issues than they are really questioning whether you are effectively doing your job.

Before your boss figures out your issues, communicate and demonstrate that you have a plan to proactively address them yourself. Remember, the best defence is an offence.

Tip #13: Time - It's Your Only Finite Resource

You can always get more promotional dollars. You can always get additional sales people. But you can never get more time in a day, week or month.

Where you invest your time will determine in part your success. Ask yourself which activities are going to positively impact revenue? Going to meetings? Paperwork? NO, NO and NO! There's only so much time in a day, use it wisely!

Tip #14: In Times of Adversity: You Need to Win Their Hearts!

In times of adversity you need to win the hearts of your sales people before you win their minds. The rapid pace of change in organizations today results in sales people needing to *believe* in the changes and their future within the organization. You need to re-recruit your good people and make them feel that they are an important part of the new organization.

Tip #15: You Can Never Over Communicate

During a cycle of change, you need to clearly and concisely communicate where the organization is heading to help your sales people understand the future. What does the new structure look like? What are the new roles and responsibilities of the team members? Discuss the rationale for the change.

In times of change do 3 things: Communicate, communicate and communicate!

Tip #16: Where There is Smoke There is an Inferno

Sales reps have incredible autonomy and latitude in their jobs. They hold positions of trust but occasionally you will come across a sales rep that may be cheating on mileage, expenses or sales calls. This is a sign that they have breached not only your trust but, the trust of the company.

In my experience, if you smell smoke it usually means there is a fire raging. If you find a breach don't stop. If you dig deeper you will find 10 more issues that you never even suspected.

Tip #17: Trust Your Own Instincts

What I have learned in my many years of coaching is that a majority of sales managers have a good sense what their issues are and how to resolve them. The problem is, they second-guess themselves out of action.

You need to trust your own instincts and act accordingly.

Tip #18: Know Your Role to Succeed

Many sales organizations struggle with a fundamental question: What is the role of the front-line sales manager? Many sales executives define it as driving sales results or "bringing in the numbers." This is true, but the question remains, "how do I do this?"

Your role is not about delivering the sales numbers; your role is about selecting, developing and retaining top sales performers. If you can effectively do all three you will have successfully realised your role as a sales manager.

Are you ready to take on your biggest challenge?

Chapter 3: Achieving Success

"You were born to win, but to be a winner, you must plan to win, prepare to win, and expect to win."

Zig Ziglar, author, salesman, and motivational speaker

Chapter 3: Achieving Success

The road to success for a sales manager is paved with potholes. In this chapter I will share with you the tips that have helped me become successful in my career. I live and die by the principles of goal setting and focus. In your role as a manager, no one is going to motivate you or give you a slap on the back. It is in many ways a thankless job. The key to success is to define in very specific terms what success looks like and having the internal motivation to achieve your goals.

It's up to you. Love the job and have fun doing it.

Tip #19: Success is Achieving the Goals You Set for Yourself

We all strive for success. Yet many people feel that they are not successful because someone has a bigger house, fancier car or more money. I believe success is measured in setting and achieving the goals you set for yourself. It is internally motivated. To achieve the success you desire, you need to set goals, work hard and stay focused.

Tip #20: Focus and Success

I was fortunate to have been promoted into seven different roles over a five-year period, moving from a sales rep to a VP of three divisions. My secret to success in each role was to figure out the 2 or 3 key success factors (KSF) and making sure my team did those 2-3 KSFs not just adequately, but extremely well.

Tip #21: Hire a Coach

As with most great athletes and winners, the key to success is having an ongoing performance coach to encourage and inspire you to excellence. Who helps you in your pursuit of coaching excellence? The first step is to hire a performance coach to help you achieve your true potential.

Tip #22: Be a STAR - Don't Fight it

Chances are you're a type "A" personality; you are driven and highly competitive. These are great traits that have helped you be successful in the field. In fact, many of the sales managers I have worked with want to be recognised by their companies as a STAR - don't fight it.

The brightest stars are those who shine for the benefit of others.

Tip #23: Having Fun is #1

Sales is a fast-paced, high-pressure profession. STAR sales managers who create an environment of fun will get more out of their teams. Engagement is about creating good feelings with the people we work for and with. There is nothing wrong with hard work unless you forget to play as well.

Sales reps that have fun produce more sales.

Tip #24: Be Authentic

People want to know the real you. Trying to be someone different will not endear you to your reps. "Be" real and people will respond to you authentically.

Tip #25: Love What You Do and Do What You Love

Sales management requires passion and full investment. If you don't love it then don't do it. I would rather be a passionate rep then a dispassionate manager. If you love the role then let the world know it.

Tip #26: Listen, Learn and Laugh a Lot

Follow these 3 L's and you will win more friends, gain knowledge and ultimately be happier.

Tip #27: Manage Your Own Motivation

Welcome to management. As a rep you lived in a highly supportive environment. In management the environment is less supportive and filled with stress. It is incumbent on you to stay inspired so you can inspire your sales people. The word **inspiration** comes from the Latin word "spiarae" which means to breathe, to live. I have found that there are many ways to keep oneself motivated. You can read a leadership book or take a leadership course. Make sure you take care of yourself, take mental health days, exercise and eat well.

Regardless which options you choose, it is essential that you stay inspired because your people need your energy as a source of motivation.

Are you clear on what you need to do to be successful this year?

Chapter 4: STARS & Bad Apples

"I mean, there's no arguing. There is no anything. There is no beating around the bush. "You're fired" is a very strong term."

Donald Trump, business magnate, television personality and author.

Chapter 4: STARS & Bad Apples

In Jim Collins book "Good to Great" he finds that the best companies have the right people in the right seats. Hiring is a very important activity for a sales manager. If you make the right decision you will not only improve the performance of the territory, but potentially elevate the performance of your team.

Sales managers face incredible pressure when hiring. The fear of vacant territories places a lot of stress on the manager to quickly hire a rep to fill the vacancy. The time associated with developing an inexperienced sales rep and getting them up to speed often seems like a poor choice. Who wants to invest the time? Because novice reps make experienced reps look much better, there is a tendency to hire people who are like you or that you like, this unfortunately jeopardizes your objectivity.

On the flip side, the pressures of admitting that you cannot save a non performing sales rep or that you have made a bad hiring decision can make firing difficult. Coupled with all the documentation and various performance plans required by your HR department, the final firing can take anywhere from 3-6 months, thereby prolonging the agony.

In my tips below I want to share with you my best insights and knowledge in the areas of hiring and firing. Both are necessary to take your team to the next level. Make the right decisions and you will be golden.

Tip #28: Being Systematic is Key

Adopting and following a consistent, multi-step hiring process will ensure that you recognize the top performers from the middle performers.

- Know what a top performer looks like at your company.
- Use a standard list of questions.
- Dig deep for specifics.
- Use psychometric profiles.

Be systematic when hiring and you will have far better outcomes.

Tip #29: Be Scientific

One of the most important parts of a sales manager's job is hiring. Many managers claim they rely on their gut instincts when making hiring decisions. I think this is an excuse for not developing and following detailed hiring profiles.

There is no excuse for hiring badly, especially when there are many fine assessment tools available, tools which have been validated over millions of reps. There is a science to hiring top performers, it's not all instinct despite claims otherwise.

Tip #30: Avoid the Plug and Play

OK, you have two candidates that you really like. One knows the products, customers and the industry. The other candidate is passionate, driven and eager to prove themself. The easy answer for a busy manager is to hire the sales rep that comes with all the experience. But have you thought about what else they bring to the table? Have you considered the infamous industry baggage?

The experienced rep may be easier on the manager for the first 6 months whereas the driven rep will have a slower start, but in 6 months he/she will likely have achieved better sales. **Hire attitude over aptitude!**

Tip #31: Fire Quickly/Hire Slowly

Many sales managers think they can save poor performing sales reps. Managers invest time and energy and usually end up frustrated and over worked. If a sales rep can't show marked improvement in 30 days then you need to consider more drastic measures.

When hiring, be systematic and proceed with caution. The better defined and consistent the process, the better your hiring decisions.

Tip #32: Cut Out the Cancer Before it Spreads

I don't care about performance. If you have a sales rep that is toxic to you and the team in terms of attitude and behaviour then you have a cancer. Bad attitudes and negativity are contagious and bring the team down. If, after several discussions the negativity continues to grow, then you need to cut the cancer out! Nothing builds team morale like a good firing of a toxic personality!

What are you doing to make sure you hire only top performers and move on your bad apples?

Chapter 5: Team Inspiration

"Leadership: the art of getting someone else to do something you want done because he wants to do it."

Dwight D. Eisenhower, the 34th President of the United States

Chapter 5: Team Inspiration

Many managers desperately want to motivate their team. The fact is that true motivation is internal. There are ways to create short-term motivation, like contests and incentives, but the real question is "what can you do to inspire your team from within"? A team is composed of different types of people with different backgrounds and different goals. Not an easy mix to motivate.

What are you doing for your people? Do you understand what drives them? Do you understand how to connect with them? Do you know how to make them feel special?

Sales managers who can adapt themselves to inspire each of their people will not only gain their teams loyalty but win their hearts.

Tip #33: It's All About the People

One of the things you realise as a manager is that success is a function of the people you have around you. If you take care of the people issues, then the people take care of the business.

Tip #34: Show Them the Love

Sales people are driven and needy creatures. They love challenges but crave recognition and accolades. A sales manager is like a parent. Show your kids (sales reps) the love and they will perform for you.

Tip #35: Recognition is Priceless

Ask any rep what they want and they will tell you it is recognition. Incentives and contests wear thin. A simple comment like "great job" is an incredible motivator to positively impact people.

Tip #36: Personalised Messages Go the Distance

Outstanding sales managers take a few minutes out of their day to handwrite personalised notes on motivational cards. Sales people will keep these cards far longer than they will retain the money they earned on a bonus.

Want to be a STAR? Send your reps a handwritten card of recognition!

Tip #37: Connect and Stay Connected

The No. 1 reason why top-performing sales reps leave an organization is their relationship – or the lack of it -- with their manager. Make sure you maintain a strong relationship with your top performers. Know them and grow them. Energize and inspire them. Great frontline sales managers do a far better job retaining top performing salespeople.

Tip #38: Create Moments of Magic

When you speak to your reps they won't remember what you said, but they will remember how you made them feel. After spending a day in the field together they will either feel drained or inspired. This is your opportunity to create what I call "moments of magic." Moments where reps feel energized and enthused. Create a moment of magic and your reps will look forward to your next encounter with anticipation and positivity.

Everyone likes to feel special. A moment of magic is connecting with your rep on a personal level whether it is asking them about their family, about their hobbies or passions, or talking about something that is important to them.

For example, one of my reps was an avid soccer fan. Every time I worked with him I would read up on how his favorite team was doing and made sure I struck up a conversation about this.

Creating moments of magic is easy and goes a long way to inspiring success.

Tip #39: I'm Promoted, Now What?

As a sales rep you relied on yourself to get things done. If you were successful it was a result of your efforts. Now that you have joined the ranks of management you realize that you must rely on others to get things done

Sales management is a great job except that you now have to deal with multiple sales people who all have their idiosyncrasies and baggage. It's not just about you anymore. Now you have to learn how to inspire success in other people.

Find ways to help your people shine instead of whine.

Tip #40: Treat People the Way You Like to be Treated

Sales management is about people. If your people are doing well the business will grow. When I got my first full time job after my MBA I started as a sales rep. I was so eager to get the job that I didn't negotiate my vacation or benefit plans. In fact, there was no vacation in my first year! The 5 other reps that were hired at the same time were smart enough to negotiate benefits up front. Even though in that first year I was the second best rep in the company and won rep of the year in my second year, I still had no vacation time.

The fact that I was not treated fairly on my first year has stuck with me for over 20 years. When I moved into the role of VP of Sales I never ever cheated a new hire out of vacation or other benefits. What I learned is that you need to treat people the same way you would want to be treated.

Treat your sales people well and you will win their loyalty.

Tip #41: Different Strokes for Different Folks

Each of your sales reps is unique. Therefore you need to adjust your coaching style and approach to get the very best out of each sales rep.

Figure out how get the best out of each rep and you will be a STAR.

Tip #42: The Self Doubter

The Self Doubter: A sales rep that sees and believes everything they do is wrong.

These reps are extremely challenging to coach. If you provide direct feedback it may be met with "I already do that" or reasons why they don't. The Self Doubter perceives any critiquing as weakness and personalizes it as confirmation that they are doing a horrible job!

The trick with this type of individual is to lead them through a process of self-discovery and improvement. By asking them a series of questions you can guide them through a process of self-awareness that will lead to an "ah ha" moment. This breakthrough may seem labour-intensive, but the payback is a stronger rep and increased performance.

Tip #43: The Talented Slacker

Talented Slacker: A rep that has all the talent but will not perform over and above.

We all have them and think we can fix them. We can't! We can only encourage them to do more. If, and only if, they go over and above do you provide positive reinforcement. Be careful how much time and effort you invest in this person as they can drain your energy with no ROI.

Tip #44: The Co-Dependent

Some managers equate doing a good job with helping their reps. They incorrectly believe that if the rep calls them 20 times a day, then they are really needed. Hello!! This is called, co-dependency and it is not good for you. It diverts you from focusing on what you need to do. If you have a rep who calls you more than once a day, every day, then you need to stop it. You want healthy sales reps who are self- managers.

What are you doing for your sales reps that will inspire them to do more?

Chapter 6: Driving Performance

"I think if you do something and it turns out pretty good, then you should go do something else wonderful, not dwell on it for too long. Just figure out what's next"

Steve Jobs, co-founder, chairman, and chief executive officer of Apple

Chapter 6: Driving Performance

When all is said and done the question is, how do you drive performance? How do you get the best out of everyone on your team? Learn some of my tips to driving performance. Sales managers are the foundation of the sales force. Your efforts and know-how will have a much bigger impact than you can imagine on the performance of your team.

The questions you ask, the focus you set and the environment you create all have a positive impact. Let's face it, you work hard and you want to have a positive impact on performance. So what are you waiting for? Go out and apply my last set of tips and be the driver of unsurpassed performance and optimal success!

Tip #45: Make Sure You Know

I once had a sales director tell me that everything was going well in the field. I wasn't sold, so I asked a simple question... *How do you know?* He turned red and put his head down because he really didn't know. He hadn't been in the field for the last three months! The only way to know what is really going on is to be in the trenches with your reps and customers.

Tip #46: Performance = Quantity x Quality

There is always the argument if you should push for greater quality over quantity or choose quantity over quality. I say performance is a combination of both; the quality of what the sales rep does and the amount of times they do it. It's not an either/or question, it's an "and."

Tip #47: Sources of Motivation

Sales people are motivated by two things, and two things only and it's not money.

1) The ability to do the job they are paid to do; and

2) Recognition for a job well done.

Tip #48: It's all About the Execution

Strategy sets direction. There are only so many strategies. All companies can come up with the same strategy, but great sales management is all about executing with excellence.

Tip #49: The Theory of 8

Want to execute with excellence? The Theory of 8 states that you need to repeat a message 8 times to change a behavior. Applying the Theory of 8 to sales management means repeating the goal or plan of action 8 times until everyone on the team understands and can effectively execute their part in achieving the goal.

By repeating your goal or plan 8 times you are in fact reaffirming the goal and effectively implanting it in the minds of your sales reps. You now have a communal goal. Excellence is around the corner!

Tip #50: Beware of Failure to Impact Syndrome

Time and time again I have seen it. Sales reps going through their daily activities like robots. They have little impact on each call, they just show up and expect the business. I call this **"failure to impact syndrome."** It is contagious and can spread throughout an entire sales force. It works as long as the business grows. Everyone gets high fives and there is no need to dig any deeper.

But what happens when sales are down and senior management starts asking questions? Sales managers struggle to come up with the answers and reps get nervous.

The cure: Get out in the field and inspire your reps to be innovative.

Tip #51: Don't Look Back, Focus Forward!

Quarterly business reviews (QBR) should be a time to get inspired and focused. The problem that I have seen is that 80% of the time spent on a QBR is focused on what has happened and 20% on what is coming next. At review time it's too late to impact the past quarter as most sales people cannot give you a straight answer on the why.

The most effective formula for QBR's is 20% on what happened and 80% on what you are going to do next quarter to drive the business. You want your sales people charged up and ready to make a difference over the next 3 months. Charge them up by focusing their thoughts and efforts on what's now and what's next.

Tip #52: Raise the Bar on Performance

All sales managers dream of having a high performance sales team. They unfortunately focus on what's going wrong and why. I suggest having quarterly business reviews where you need to raise the bar each and every time. What is critical in this process is to consistently ask the same question: "What do you need to do to get to x% of quota?"

If the sales rep is at 120% of quota I would ask *"what do you need to do to get to 125%?"*

If the sales rep is at 95% of quota then ask *"what do you need to do to get to 100%?"*

By consistently asking the same question your reps will learn to come prepared with ideas and initiatives that will enable them to reach the next level.

What are you going to do differently to drive performance?

Conclusion:

We have come to the end of the book and you have taken the first step in seeking out the resources you require to be the best sales leader you can be.

My hope is that you have realised that you are the KEY to the success of your organization. As the coach and leader of your team you are the difference between mediocre and stellar results.

Given the importance of your role, I hope that you have begun to understand that you need to continuously improve your skill set. My intentions are that **52 Sales Management Tips** serves as a stepping-stone in learning and developing in how to become a GREAT sales manager. Hopefully the tips that I have shared will help you through many situations, but my real goal is to inspire you to invest in yourself. The true sign of a successful manager is one who seeks out the resources that will accelerate his/her learning curve.

It doesn't matter if you are just starting out as a sales manager or you have been in this job for the last 10 years, you can always improve and achieve greater success.

My goal for you is threefold:

1. You realise that your role is to develop your sales people to achieve to their fullest potential. Effective coaching skills are the surest path to get there.

2. You understand that applying FOCUS in all aspects of your daily activities will help you become more effective. Therefore you need to focus on your coaching, business planning and time management. By distilling your focus to the 2-3 most impactful activities you will achieve the success you desire.

3. Lastly, by applying my tips you will become a more confident sales manager.

Get out in the field, have fun, make lots of money and inspire your people to be their best. You have the potential to be the best sales manager in your company.

Wishing you ongoing success,

Steven Rosen

Steven Rosen
CEO STAR Results
Author, Executive Sales Coach, Speaker

Acknowledgments:

This book would not have happened without the great editing, words of encouragement and an occasional push received from my friend Michelle Bloomberg, Editor at Your Service. www.editoratyourservice.com/.

I often quote the ground breaking research that the CEB has done in the area of front line sales management coaching. It is a must read for all sales executives and managers.

"World-Class Sales Coaching - Building a First-Line Manager Coaching Program" 2007.

About Steven Rosen:

Steven Rosen, is a sales management expert who transforms sales managers into great sales coaches. Steven works with sales executives to hire better reps and managers, develop sales teams that outperform the competition, and by doing so achieve greater personal and professional success.

He has authored many articles in the areas of sales management coaching and training. He is a regular contributor to a variety of sales web sites and writes a sales management blog called, *Stirring it Up*.

Steven's mission is to inspire sales leaders, managers and reps to achieve their full business potential. When you hire Steven, you get Steven. He has a hands-on approach and thrives on working directly with his clients in helping them to discover and achieve their vision.

Steven knows sales -- inside and out. He's been in the trenches and commanded the troops. Steven builds high performance teams, mentoring senior sales executives and front line sales managers to grow their businesses to new heights.

His results orientated approach to corporate leadership, strategy development, execution and building high performance teams in the pharmaceutical and packaged goods sectors defined his success. His expertise in aligning sales and marketing initiatives to achieve key business results and exceed customer expectations has delivered STAR Results from his days as a sales rep to his tenure as a VP of sales for two multi-national pharmaceutical corporations.

He is a high energy and colourful speaker who will inspire your organization to realise **STAR Results**. Skip the learning curve, and let Steven motivate you to achieve the balance and success you deserve.

If you are ready to achieve STAR results through a personalized program of leadership coaching, contact Steven at steven@starresults.com or 905-737-4548.

66959325R00040

Made in the USA
Middletown, DE
09 September 2019